# COMMITTED TO LOVE:

## *Caring for Same-Sex Christian Couples*

**Reverend Brice Thomas**

*Dedication*

To all gay and lesbian couples who have the courage to stay together in spite of their relationship disputes, societal pressures, churches that oppress and/or families that disown them. The Good News is…it will get better. God's love and acceptance of you is absolute. You can count on it.

## Preface and Acknowledgements

There are several people I want to thank and acknowledge for the text you have in your hands today. I started this research over 15 years ago as I began my studies in Conflict Resolution at the former McGregor School of Antioch University in Yellow Springs, Ohio in 1996. At that time I was certain my thesis, "Conflict Structures in Gay and Lesbian Relationships" would be featured on Oprah's book club, and eventually become a NY Times best seller. However, the inner conflict I was experiencing around issues of shame and internalized homophobia in my own life were too heavy to see the project through. There were some in the program who were even uncomfortable with the subject matter, and I found difficulty gaining support for this research. I eventually dropped out of the program. Just the thought that this sensitive research could be so simply dismissed because it caused someone to be "uncomfortable" nearly destroyed my own sense of achievement and worthiness. Even I didn't believe how important this work really was.

Later my research was rekindled when I began seminary in 2002 after much encouragement and support by Rev. Timothy Forbess, my good friend and mentor in ministry. I decided to rewrite my thesis for a class on pastoral care and counseling. My professor, Dr. Anne McWilliams, was such a godsend in every sense of the word. She not only supported my work, but pushed me to discover a spiritual foundation for my writing. I was relatively new to the church again, having been invited back into relationship with God through a United Church of Christ pastor, Rev. Dr. Mike Castle, and his congregation. Cross Creek Community Church in Centerville, Ohio was my oasis; the spiritual home for which I had always longed, and the reconnection to God I so desperately desired. Cross Creek allowed me to "test" my thesis and gather information from their gay and lesbian congregants through workshops and interviews, all the while healing me from the disdain, homophobia and self-hatred I had learned from the Christian culture as an adolescent. In the midst of this academic work I realized that I was really just trying to work out my own experiences of exclusion through research and writing, and also to understand the conflict issues I was having in my significant relationship.

So I set my research aside for a few years and launched a new UCC church after ordination in 2005. Soon I began officiating commitment ceremonies and realized there was a real need for a pre-commitment counseling program for the couples I was marrying. So I dusted off my research and organized my writings into a five-session program called, "Committed to Love: Pastoral Care for Same-Sex Couples." I used the program often with much success. But it wasn't until I met a wonderful friend and kindred spirit named Kelly Basinger who would help me take this program to the next level of publishing. For all of the folks who traveled with me on this journey, even those who were uncomfortable with my research, I say thank you! For even the challenge to overcome obstacles along the way taught me to jump higher and stretch further for the finish line.

I have also written an introduction for pastors who just don't know where to begin with supporting the gay and lesbian couples in their churches. I trust that you will take the time to discern your own beliefs about homosexuality and same-sex coupling. I believe that God calls us to minister to whoever comes to us, and not differentiate who is worthy of our care. Did Jesus ever reject someone who needed healing? He may have initially turned some away (i.e. the woman he called a dog in Matthew 15), but even Jesus learned to love the outcast. So should we!

The first section of the workbook introduces clergy to a psychosystematic approach to pastoral care. It is a rather brief summary of two beneficial resources that have helped me reorient my perspective of caring for gay and lesbian couples; Larry Kent Graham's *Care of Persons, Care of Worlds* (Abingdon Press) and David K. Switzer's *Pastoral Care of Gays, Lesbians, and Their Families* (Fortress Press). I highly recommend deeper reading of these two resources for pastors who just don't know where to begin with supporting the gay and lesbian couples in their churches. This section will help pastors discern their own beliefs about homosexuality and same-sex coupling, and provide reflections for building a new perspective.

I also acknowledge that this program does not address all of the issues that might exist in same-sex relationships. While I have considered the influence of sex roles, homophobia, enmeshment, promiscuity, church and family dynamics on gay and lesbian relationships, I have not researched the specific issues facing intersexed, bi-sexual, transgendered or same gender loving people. I do hope that their unique needs will be addressed as the freedom to marry whoever we want will become a reality in this decade.

Namaste,
Reverend Brice A. Thomas

September, 2011

*"The task of pastoral theology is to help us recover our heritage and to recover from it."*
*John Patton*

# Pre-Counseling Reflection
# A Pastoral Response to Counseling Gays and Lesbians

## Introduction To Psychosystematic Pastoral Care

## The Pastoral Response to Caring for Gay and Lesbian Persons

## Homophobia and Heterosexism

## Going to the Dogs

# Counseling Sessions

# Introduction to Psychosystematic Pastoral Care

## *A New Paradigm For Counseling Issues Of Sexual Orientation*

An important step in tackling the issues of sexuality is to work from a paradigm that better explains the psyche of the gay or lesbian person, and fully presents the systemic environment by which that psyche has been shaped and influenced. Like Patton's statement in the introduction of his book, appropriate "pastoral theology is the means by which we recover our heritage and recover from its misuse or misunderstanding."[1] Working from this definition, five major sources of knowledge and experience are recommended for creating psychosystematic theory and developing guidelines for pastoral care.

These five sources of knowledge and experience are:
- practicing the ministry of care;
- understanding the social and cultural contexts in which the ministry occurs;
- identifying the living religious traditions contextualizing the ministry;
- incorporating relevant secular knowledge into the development of theory and practice; and
- recognizing the individual personhood of the caretaker and pastoral theologian carrying out the act of ministry.

---

1.  Larry Kent Graham, *Care of Persons, Care of Worlds* (Nashville: Abingdon Press, 1992), p. 21.

Why change one's perspective for doing counseling? Dr. Larry Graham believes that "pastoral theology must expand its theoretical foundations and practical responses in the light of more contextual and systemic resources."[2] This pre-counseling reflection describes the common and historical responses to situations of care, identifies the problematic nature of these responses and prescribes an alternative use of systemic analysis for enhanced resolution.

## *Transforming Care: Linking Psyches and Systems*

Individual bias is a lens that all pastoral caretakers and theologians use to understand and analyze issues of care, and offer appropriate ministry to care seekers. It is significant how permanently we are connected to our environment and how that systemic relationship affects our ability or inability to realize self-fulfillment. Ultimately, these systemic elements constitute powerful forces that can contribute to intense pain and suffering. Our individual biases are also a result of these elements and often require a broader understanding of systems theory and evaluation of the models historically used to practice care giving.

### Historical Worldviews of Pastoral Care

The dominant orientation has been an existentialist-anthropological model and focuses on the health and fulfillment of individual persons. Emphasis on self-realization, fulfillment and individual growth supersedes more social and communal viewpoints. It can be characterized by four world views.

The first is an internalized locus of control and responsibility, where "the individual, rather than the system, is blamed when things do not work out."[3] This plays out in ministry when pastoral counselors suggest that people must take responsibility for their own actions and improve their condition through their

2.  Ibid., p. 23.
3.  Ibid., p. 33.

own individual efforts. This approach tends to be punitive and oppressive for people who have less power for self-realization.

A second type of world view is an external locus of control and internal locus of responsibility. In this view individuals and groups believe they are responsible for their own situations, even though they have no control over them. Those who are disadvantaged are that way because of character flaws or lack of motivation. Marginalization is a product of an individual's inability to take responsibility for one's environment.

The third view results from external control and external responsibility, such as being enslaved by someone else. Helplessness at achieving personal goals might be interpreted as passive, dependent, or cowardly.

The final view is characterized by an externalized locus of responsibility and internalized locus of control. Environment in this view is not due to one's inabilities, but that change could happen if given the opportunity. Persons from racial and ethnic minorities may see their problems not resulting from themselves, but from external forces. Change happens when activism occurs in context of communal participation rather than from individual means.

These four world views have framed the practice of pastoral care and counseling prior to 1960. Since then many authors have sought to offer alternative models for ministry. Process theology, transgenerational concepts of relatedness, central emphasis on selfhood, liberation theology, ethical egoism and humanistic psychology are some theories that have attempted to subvert the dominant existentialist-anthropological models. These theories, while significant for changing paradigms in the field of psychotherapeutic counseling, still lack grounding in systemic thinking.

# Characteristics Of Systemic Thinking

Graham suggests that a systemic perspective emphasizes togetherness, ongoing processes and transactions, and cooperation and reciprocal influence. It affirms both/and instead of either/or, and that creative advances include what has gone before. It underscores the individual's ongoing relationship to society, culture and nature and it concerns itself with holism.[4] In the context of pastoral care and counseling, systemic thinking has four characteristics:

- it affirms the interconnection between all things and responds to persons accordingly;

- it is concerned with the structured organization of persons and of the nature of the power relationship between persons and their environments;

- it attempts to identify, stabilize, and modify the reciprocal transactions at work within individuals, and those that operate between individuals and their environments;

- and it recognizes that change is inherent in the nature of things and attempts to influence change in such a way that environments as well as individuals are enhanced.[5]

Just as integral to systems thinking in pastoral care and counseling is the demonstration of the "ongoing, permanent, and reciprocal interaction between the psyches of persons and the larger environments that are bringing psyches into being and influencing their nature. The relationship between them is synaptic, or spiritual, characterized by mutual reception, rejection, struggle, and creative accomplishment."[6] Systemic thinking characterizes the psyche, or human personality, as an open system rather than independent and non-communal. It is an active agent in the activity of experience and the creative process. It is influenced by systems, and in turn affects those very same systems. The human

4.   Ibid., p. 39.
5.   Ibid., p. 40.
6.   Ibid., p. 41.

psyche or soul then derives its identity, function and value from its participation in these systems and subsystems, and continues to evolve those systems in response. In pastoral care and counseling, such a response is the modification of these systems which in turn affects change in the larger structures of the world.

**What could be systemic influences on same-sex relationships in your local area?**

# How can I respond to these influences with pastoral care?

_____

_____

_____

_____

_____

_____

_____

_____

_____

## Principles of Psychosystematic Pastoral Care Ministry

The role of pastoral care ministry is being one of the vehicles by which God's love is affirmed and shared through two dimensions; by restoring that which is estranged to new harmony and cooperation, and promoting "new beings" in a "new creation" that are productive in new and un-imposed ways.[7] There are five principles that identify the nature of psychosystematic caregiving; organicity, simultaneity, conscientization, advocacy and adventure.

- Organicity describes the interconnections that extend backwards in family and culture and outward to the multiple influences in one's world.

- Simultaneity demands a response to the organic relationships that exists between persons and their worlds simultaneously.

- Conscientization seeks awareness of the impact that social order has on one's difficulties and assists strategic actions to neutralize, change or transform destructive elements in that social order.

- Advocacy reshapes public policies to promote a positive environment for the careseeker.

- Adventure recognizes that God's presence in this transformation is an expected gift of grace and fruit of hope.[8]

7.   Ibid., p. 44.
8.   Ibid., p. 47.

**What are some possible exercises that incorporate these pastoral care principles into counseling same-sex relationships?**

Organicity (i.e., create a family tree of familial relationships)

_____

_____

_____

Simultaneity (i.e., identify which of those branches are healthy or unhealthy) _____

_____

_____

Conscientization (i.e., describe how these unhealthy branches affect the relationship) _____

_____

_____

Advocacy (i.e., what public policies restrict our development of a healthy relationship?) _____

_____

_____

Adventure (i.e., what are some biblical narratives of God's unexpected gift of grace and hope?)_____

_____

_____

A psychosystematic model for pastoral care and counseling identifies a ministry that is purposed to increase the love of self, God and neighbor by developing the capacity to work for a just social order in partnership with the natural order of life. It provides the context for victims and perpetrators of lovelessness, injustice and environmental disorder to engage the destructive forces of their lives in a way that brings healing, sustenance, guidance and liberation to their souls.[9] This model promises both an internal diagnostic for the care of persons, and an external view of caring for the world. It is dynamic, holistic and inclusive in its approach. It has been a framework that has significantly impacted the research, study and formation of this pastoral care and counseling ministry for gay and lesbian persons.

**What is my responsibility as pastoral caregiver to same-sex couples?**

_____

_____

_____

_____

_____

_____

_____

_____

_____

9.   Ibid., p. 48.

# The Pastoral Response to Caring for Gay and Lesbian Persons

## *Overcoming Fear: the Realities of Pastoral Care*

Clergy who reject the opportunities to embrace their gay and lesbian laity may do so because of their religious belief system or for fear of treading into unknown territory. This pre-counseling session offers practical insights for heterosexual clergy to overcome their fears and beliefs, encouraging them to respond to their call as pastoral caregivers. It also offers this same challenge to gay and lesbian clergy, framing the discussion around the dynamics of their sexual orientation in the midst of ministry.

The first reality about pastoral care and counseling of gays and lesbians by clergy is that very few are knowingly doing much of it. The second reality, however, is that a large percentage of clergy are unknowingly doing it quite often. Gays and lesbians are a vital, dynamic and integrated part of many, many congregations. But like so many gays and lesbians in society, they are serving their churches in the closet. This makes the church's ministry to them incomplete and hindered.[10] How can clergy help tear down walls of homophobia and heterosexism so that they may be better caregivers? The question isn't, do you want to? The question is, how will you respond to your call as minister of the gospel to all people?

10. David K. Switzer, *Pastoral Care of Gays, Lesbians, and Their Families* (Minneapolis: Fortress Press, 1999), p. 66.

11

# What do I believe theologically about homosexuality?

_____

_____

_____

_____

_____

_____


# How do I feel about homosexual behavior?

_____

_____

_____

_____

_____

_____

How have I been trained to respond to gays and lesbians?

How can I be helpful without being hypocritical?

Allow love to flow through you!

# *The Impact of the Personhood of the Pastor*

It is clear that, "both the words and overt behavior of Jesus in his obedience to God, thus revealing what God wants of us, do not allow us to fail to respond to or to seek out persons who need our caring ministry regardless of who they are, what their needs are, our opinions about them, whether we like them or not, or whether we are comfortable with the person or that type of person or with that sort of situation. We are called to engage ourselves with any person or persons as we attempt faithfully to represent Christ."[11] That doesn't mean that anxiety, discomfort or lack of confidence shouldn't exist in the midst of these caregiving situations. All of us possess flaws, insecurities, and uncertainties that may interfere with our effectiveness as pastoral caregivers. But does that dismiss our responsibility to respond to a call for pastoral care or counseling?

Who we are as persons may affect our ability to effectively express our caring as persons and ministerial professionals. But regardless, pastoral care is "not just doing something for, to, or in the presence of others; it is a demonstrative proclamation of the love of God as it was so concretely, clearly and powerfully demonstrated in Jesus the Christ. We represent Christ as the human beings we are. But effective pastoral caring depends on our ability to establish personal relationships that are characterized and empowered by intimacy."[12] Being self-aware and open to self-disclosure as a pastoral caregiver is necessary in order that counselees can be and do the same. It's not enough to admit that you are unprepared or inexperienced to deal with situations where you lack the intimacy to follow through. We all have embedded prejudice that limits our effectiveness. The impediments to effective ministry are real but not enduring.

---

11. Ibid.
12. Ibid., p. 67.

# What gifts and skills do I bring to this counseling situation?

_____

_____

_____

_____

_____

_____

_____

# What hindrances do I also bring with me?

_____

_____

_____

_____

_____

_____

_____

## *Impediments to Ministry with Gays and Lesbians*

Homophobia and heterosexism define the fundamental impediments to effective pastoral care and counseling with gays and lesbians. The literal meaning and the contemporary meaning of homophobia are quite contradictory. Homophobia literally means the "fear of sameness," but is commonly understood as "same sex." It has become synonymous with prejudice, anger, hatred and discrimination. Our entire society is organized by heterosexuality. Society's structure and subsequent support systems have been constructed to serve the majority heterosexual populace. It's not surprising then that anything that is a minority in this system; whether it is defined by race, class, culture or sexual orientation, will be considered different and abnormal. But difference and abnormality has historically led to "discrimination, often anger and hatred, sometimes violence, with the extreme being genocide. The people who are in the majority always want to keep the people of the minority separate, apart, down underneath if possible. We see it in every country in the world. Their being different (that is, from us) is a threat to us."[13] The intensity might lessen with justice and reform, but social ostracism, the lack of desire to understand or be close, exclusiveness, and discriminatory laws continue to separate and create barriers. Gays and lesbians continue to experience these attitudes in their daily lives, by government, society, family, and church. This is heterosexism.

13. Ibid., p. 69.

17

How will I overcome my own impediments to this ministry of care?

_____

_____

_____

_____

_____

_____

_____

What are the advantages for embracing this care situation in my ministry?

_____

_____

_____

_____

_____

_____

_____

# What are the disadvantages?

when you are
present in this
moment, you
break the
continuity of

your
of
past

story.

and
future.

then true intelligence
arises, and also love.

→ Eckhart Tolle

# Homophobia and Heterosexism

This is the point: if we're going to be Christ's servants to anyone in need (being a neighbor to our neighbor), then it is our Lord who calls us to change our attitudes and feelings and who can assist us in doing it. In fact, such change is called for, along with our being saved from racism, sexism, social classism, and other spiritual limitations if we're to become more fully Christian. Merely being ordained or being in some other designated Christian vocation does not blot out all of our transgressions, among them our often unconscious biases.[14]

## *Gay Clergy*

Gay or lesbian pastors may have a head start in dealing with homophobia or heterosexism, but often do not have experience with pastoral care and counseling of gay and lesbian parishioners. Being closeted themselves, feeling attracted to same-sex members of the congregation, premature reassuring of homosexual orientations and issues surrounding appropriate intimacy in the midst of these relationships are issues that can impede effective pastoral functioning. Being accountable to a competent experienced psychotherapist or another pastor in whom they have confidence can help them grow in their own personal and professional lives. It is equally important for them to use their self-awareness for developing the insight and well-being of the counselee.

14. Ibid., p. 71.

**For Gay Clergy:**
How will I respond to this ministry of care?

_____

_____

_____

_____

_____

_____

_____

What issues does this counseling situation bring up in my own life?

_____

_____

_____

_____

_____

_____

_____

_____

## *Heterosexual Clergy*

The heterosexual pastor should also work to identify past experiences that have framed their homophobia and confront the structures of heterosexism in their ministry. They also must identify their convictions as being helpful or a hindrance. Even the pastor who believes homosexual behavior is wrong can still be compassionate, skillful, and helpful to the gay or lesbian person. It is not what they believe that can block a helpful pastoral relationship, but how they feel and how their feelings shape what they say and how they say it. They must be conscious of not getting trapped by their stereotyping of gays or lesbians. The first step toward effective counseling is looking beyond the stereotype and getting to know the person. The next step is then to understand the most helpful pastoral approach in a counseling situation, and when and how to express their convictions.[15]

**For Straight Clergy:**
**How will I respond to this ministry of care?**

_____

_____

_____

_____

_____

_____

_____

15. Ibid., pp. 76-77.

What issues does this counseling situation bring up in my own life?

_____

_____

_____

_____

_____

_____

_____

_____

## *The Christian Response*
### Hiding Behind the Bible

It is well for us pastors to realize that at some times we may declare the Bible as authoritative on a particular issue as a means of our own self-protection. The pastor who relates to people in an authoritarian manner cannot compel change in persons, even when he or she asserts the authority of the Bible. Our convictions can be a help or a hindrance to effective pastoral counseling, depending on how we express them and on the quality of our relationship with the person with whom we are talking. Therefore, the most helpful beginning point in any act of pastoral counseling is an invitation to the other person to express the most pressing feelings and/or needs of which she or he is aware right at the present moment. We put away any preconceptions of the other person that we might have. We then observe perceptively and listen intently both to the precise words and their explicit meanings as well as to any possible implicit meaning.[16]

**What biblical texts are problematic for my non-judgemental approach to counseling in this situation?**

---

16. Ibid., p. 78.

## The Truth of God's Love

Clergy who feel or believe that they cannot, or won't counsel with gay and lesbian persons, couples and families must ask themselves then, what is the Christian response? What must be maintained in our minds is this fundamental truth; God loves everyone and pastors represent to gays and lesbians the God of love as revealed in Jesus the Christ. We are all called as pastors to reflect that truth, and that truth must be reflected without condemnation, even though our beliefs and feelings might be disapproving. This truth of God's love may be evidenced through knowing and recommending resources in the community or by referring counselees to competent and experienced pastors or professional psychotherapists. The truth of God's love begins by answering the call to help anyone in need within the range of our abilities. That truth can bring freedom to do God's work, whether it is in or through us.

What responses or recommendations will I give for same-sex couples seeking counseling?

_____

_____

_____

_____

_____

_____

_____

_____

_____

_____

## Going to the Dogs

This truth of God's love, as revealed through Jesus Christ, had not completely evolved until later in his ministry. Even Jesus had to face his own prejudices and exclusionary behavior. One compelling biblical narrative to this point is his exchange with the Canaanite woman in Matthew 15:21-28.

*Jesus left that place and went away to the district of Tyre and Sidon. Just then a Canaanite woman from that region came out and started shouting, "Have mercy on me, Lord, Son of David; my daughter is tormented by a demon." But he did not answer her at all. And his disciples came and urged him, saying, "Send her away, for she keeps shouting after us." He answered, "I was sent only to the lost sheep of the house of Israel." But she came and knelt before him, saying, "Lord, help me." He answered, "It is not fair to take the childrens' food and throw it to the dogs." She said, "Yes, Lord, yet even the dogs eat the crumbs that fall from their masters' table." Then Jesus answered her, "Woman, great is your faith! Let it be done for you as you wish." And her daughter was healed instantly. (NRSV)*

While I was growing up, my family had a pet dog named Barney. He was a stray we found resting under an old abandoned tractor on the farm where we often went to buy fresh vegetables in the summer. Barney was our most favorite pet. With predominant beagle DNA in his blood, he was a gentle, fun-loving pet that could entertain us for hours in the backyard, endearing us with his fog-horn like howl, his droopy ears, and sad puppy dog eyes. But Mom was very firm with her restrictions. Barney had to stay outside during the day. He could not eat table scraps, and he must be walked and washed on a regular basis. After it became evident that Barney suffered from epilepsy, a disease common to many mixed breeds, he was allowed into the house more frequently later in his life; but she was firm on the rule that he could not be fed from the table.

Such began the relationship with my own purebred beagle years later. BJ was her name, which was short for Barney Junior. She was a gift to my partner on his 35th birthday. And even though her cute puppy looks could melt the iciest heart, we also stood firm with the rules. No table scraps, no begging at meals. But BJ knew just what slight degree the rules could be bent. And so when dinner was ready each evening she would take her place right at our feet; a good place to stretch one direction or another to grab whatever stray crumb might fall during the meal!

Then as time went by, the table rules got bent a little more. She was so much a part of us, more and more not just a domestic breed. She understood our speech and we came to understand her much fuller vocabulary of whimper, posture, body language, claw, touch, nudge, stare, ear twitch. And so at breakfast each morning, BJ eventually got a bit of toast and at the end of dinner, a choice bite of meat saved for her from my own plate. If I lingered too long before offering it, I would notice a furry snout delicately laid on my knee—just a reminder.

She lived heartily for six years, and then suddenly her kidneys began to fail long before she had ever come near old age. Months later, when she lost her appetite for the dog food she had always relished, the rules became irrelevant. Mealtime became an inventory of the refrigerator. Whatever she would eat, she could have: bread, steak, chicken and rice, and dog biscuits at any time of day. When she became too tired to bend and eat from her dish on the floor, then she got it from our hands. And when nothing else appealed any more, we nourished her from an IV. We were determined that she would live if we just kept on trying.

Missing her as we do, I look back now over the nine years since her death and realize what happened: gradually she changed my mind about the restrictions we imposed on the way she was fed, and our "table rules" were slowly dissolved and eventually eliminated. I found myself turning around, letting go of all our rules, all our contrived distinctions; knowing that what was important was not that she be differentiated from us like some lesser creature; but that her life had been nourished. BJ's lovely life had changed me; so much that I would have lifted her up onto the table if only it had meant that she could eat to live one more day.

It was another "dog" who changed Jesus' mind as well. As one of the earliest inhabitants of the pagan region of Tyre and Sidon, the Canaanite was known to be the worst of the lot, a hardened pagan, a longtime enemy. And this one, the disciples saw as a real cur: A woman—and an unescorted woman at that, a woman whose undoubtedly shady past must surely have caused the demonic possession in the family; a woman brazen enough to initiate conversation with a man. Jesus is silent in the face of her. The disciples, however, have their prayer shawls in a knot: Get rid of her, they urge, "Do what she wants, so she'll get out of our hair."

But Jesus responds, "No; I wasn't sent for her." Then, this "dog" who is satisfied just to be under the table proceeds to change his heart. She is not beholden to the "official rules" or even to Jesus' understanding of his own vocation, but insists that she and her daughter have a right to healing. She doggedly reminds Jesus that he is not after all servant of the "official religion" or of biblical tradition, but of an uncontrollable Spirit who blows where she will blow, touches whom she will touch, beckons whom she will beckon, heals whom she will heal.

The Jesus we meet before this incident shows partiality to his own people, distinguishing between insiders and outsiders. This Jesus is a problem, if your theology demands perfection in a savior. I too have wrestled with him: precisely because of what He taught us, I shudder at his initial responses. But you know something? In the end, this incident endears him to me more. Here is no brittle, paper-doll Messiah, but one challenged as we are: one who shares our condition and is not ashamed to correct himself. Because just then, this "Son of David" remembers who he is. He comes back to himself in a new way. He admits, as if it were the most natural thing in the world (and of course, it is), that he had been wrong and had his mind changed.

In a sense, it is Jesus' own awakening that takes him far beyond first-century Palestine's "honor culture." Jesus does not save face. He is challenged by the woman on his own terms—by her living, pushy faith—to make room for outcast and alien. It's a profound conversion for him: continue reading in this gospel, and watch how his encounters have a shifted nuance, his stories a new and pronounced bias for the poor and the outsider. There is an insight threading its way through the rest of Matthew that traces back to the argument of a Canaanite "dog."

Being a faithful people is all about changing the table rules and getting changed yourself! It's about who gets to be at the table, and who will be at the table in spite of us; and thereby about the social implications for relations between poor and non-poor, genders, sexual orientations, abilities, pedigrees. It is about a banquet for dogs. Suddenly the persona of the God enfleshed in Jesus does not only have to do with chosen people. Not only with purebreds—Shelties and Great Danes and German Shorthaired Pointers—but with mongrels. Mutts. Half-breeds and Heinz 57s. The ones that track mud into our sanctuaries and shake pond water all over our doctrine, who hungrily snarf up any little morsel that falls and don't know how to sit and stay. The secret we must all discover from outsiders like the Canaanite woman is that if we hold their name up to a mirror, we come face to face with the Holy name. And those we wrote off as "dogs" become revealers of God.

I have four other dogs now, two mixed-breed hounds named Riley and Millie, a feisty Rat Terrier named Buddy, and two extremely high strung Jackapoos (half Jack Russell Terrier and half Toy Poodle) named, Jack and Pooh. In a lot of ways BJ blazed the way for these puppies; we relentlessly spoil them. And I wonder what it's like for them to sit at my feet during dinner time. From down there, you can't see the whole spread, only the rim of a plate, perhaps whatever is lying within a few inches of the edge. It makes you hungry. But with faith, and a good nose, you can imagine the truth: there is more than crumbs there, for a little dog with the temerity to sit close.

Many churches are on the verge of reaching out to members of their community that some may regard as beneath them on the economic ladder of success. Ministry work with marginalized people–the homeless, low income neighborhoods, and disenfranchised segments of society–will bring folks into our churches that we might not normally invite into our club. They won't value our traditions, they won't idolize our worship space, and they won't take the gospel at face value. They will be looking for more than crumbs from our table. And we'll need to be ready to give them the best that we have. It is the kind of thing that must happen to each and every one of us. For even one sharp word or unapproving glance will negate the gospel that we preach.

We have to turn our priorities around, let go of all our rules, all our contrived distinctions; knowing that what is important is not that they be differentiated from us; but that their lives must be nourished. We need to turn our criticism onto ourselves. It can be a shock, of course, to realize what we have been doing all along. Our habitual way of camouflaging ourselves has been stripped away. No longer can we make other people responsible for our own shortcomings. We begin to see other people as they really are and ourselves as we really are. We come to our moment of truth the way Jesus came to his.

May the mark of our lives and ministries be this: that we are not too proud to go sit under the table for a bit, listen to the language of the outsider and thereby learn about the feast of the kingdom of God that is to come. Amen.

*(Adapted from Barry J. Robinson's thoughts on the text in "Projection Withdrawal" from August 14, 2005 – www.fernstone.org, and Gail Ricciuti's sermon "God of Mongrels" from December 2, 2001 - www.csec. org/csec/sermon/ricciuti_4509.htm)*

# Recommendations for using this counseling program with same-sex couples

I developed the following counseling program to be used in a multi-session format. I have used it as a pre-marital (or pre-commitment ceremony) program; a dispute resolution workshop for groups of couples and/or individuals; and as a relationship counseling intervention for couples experiencing conflict. For couple counseling sessions, it works best to break up the appointments into five distinct sessions with the homework questions assigned between each appointment. Each session should take a minimum of one hour to cover adequately.

You also may need to adapt the program to fit the needs of the couple. For instance, my research has indicated that a majority of lesbian couples do not deal with promiscuity in their relationship. But they may need to discern the issues of monogomy for themselves. Feel free to skip this chapter for them. It will however be important for gay male couples to resolve.

Your counselees should download PDF versions of the workbook sessions for their own use (at a minimal cost) from my website, www.BriceThomas.com. I encourage each person in the relationship to have their own workbook.

Pastoral Counseling is an art in of itself. My pastoral counseling coursework in seminary was just the tip of the iceberg when introducing the issues that I would eventually encounter in the parish setting. In some counseling situations I had to be honest that I wasn't prepared for what I experienced. Sometimes I just could not meet the counseling needs of my congregants, and I was not afraid to refer them to other professionals.

The real gift of this program to clergy is that in the process of counseling your gay and lesbian congregants you will learn much about the resources available to them in your local area. There will be partnerships and alliances that you will form to support this new emerging ministry. And once word gets out that your church is open to and affirming of same-sex couples, the good news will spread. Prepare your congregations for such a time as this.

I am always available for consultation, advice or just support through my website or mail@bricethomas.com. And my prayers are with you on this journey.

Blessings!
Pastor Brice

# Session #1 - Homosexuality and the Church

## *The Christian Response*

One of the most divisive external forces against gay and lesbian couples has been, regrettably, the Christian Church. "Most of the Gay community is wary of anything connected to the word Christian lately," says Mary Jo Osterman, editor of Open Hands magazine.[17] Peter Jucha, special contributor for the Dallas Voice echoes these sentiments. "For years now, we in the gay, lesbian, transgendered and bisexual community have been coming out of our societal closets. What messages have we had from our Christian brothers and sisters? For the most part, we've been told we'd be going straight (pardon the pun) to hell."[18]

Alan P. Bell and Martin S. Weinberg cite that many writers believe Christianity is responsible for both societal homophobia and an internalized homophobia demonstrated by homosexuals. They suggest that the misinterpretation of certain Biblical passages due to the preoccupation with procreative sexuality by New Testament authors led to the renunciation of any sexual passion. They labeled any type of non-reproductive sexuality irrational and unacceptable.[19]

17. Wayne Hoffman, "The Truest of Christian Struggles: Publications for Gay Christians' Fight for Justice and Compassion," Washington Blade, 5 Jan. 1996.
18. Peter Jucha, "Gay is More Than Just Okay: Gay and Lesbian Persons Must Find a New Positive Theological Foundation for Their Lives," Dallas Voice, 7 Mar. 1997.
19. Alan Bell, Martin Weinberg, and Sue Kiefer Hammersmith, Sexual Preference: Its Development in Men and Women (Bloomington: Indiana UP, 1988), p. 149.

Although this atmosphere is changing in some mainline denominations, the seeds of past oppression and ostracism may still have an impact on a gay or lesbian person's identity as a Christian.

**How have I been judged by other Christians?**

_____

_____

_____

_____

_____

_____

_____

_____

This oppressive view of sex by religion has created the common characteristic of guilt among homosexuals. Jucha says that, "Even after leaving the religions that oppressed gays, many still continue to operate with a void where the guilty and oppressive feelings once were. Because the only bases of substance that they've ever had were the guilty and oppressive feelings, the only things that ever fill that void are the same old guilt and oppression."[20] Bell and Weinberg found that homosexuals who remained active in their oppressive religious communities had much more conflict in their relationships than those who had "renounced" their religious heritage. Additional researchers have found that religious homosexuals had extremely low levels of self-esteem and tended to feel alienated from others.[21] A product of this religious guilt is rejection. These feelings affect the gay or lesbian's future relationship as rejection perpetuates rejection. "There is a tendency to go for those who will reject us or to do unto others as has been done unto us--to reject them. The damage from early rejection and the perpetuation of the cycle in adult relationships is often devastating to the capacity to develop positive long-term relationships."[22]

20. Jucha.
21. Bell, p. 150.
22. Andrea L. T. Peterson, "Dr. Richard Discusses the Value and Difficulties of Gay Relationships," *Dallas Voice*, 14 Jun. 1996.

How has that judgment affected my relationship with God?

_____

_____

_____

_____

_____

_____

Has my view of morality or ethics changed because of this? In what ways?

_____

_____

_____

_____

_____

_____

_____

How do I include God in my relationship with my partner?

_____

_____

_____

_____

_____

_____

_____

_____

_____

Love is the
absence of
judgement.

— Tenzin Gyatso

* Bonus! Apply this idea once
today and see how it changes
your world!

# Learning the Truth (from a letter to a sibling)

Dear Sister,

It was good to speak with you on the phone. Life has been extremely busy for me these past six months with graduate school and the new job. In fact, my academic studies of late have reminded me of our conversation from New Years Day about me being gay. Although I sensed that you were somewhat disenchanted with how it ended, I want to reassure you that I understand exactly where you are coming from and do not harbor any ill feelings toward you for your beliefs in what or who I am. Having spent the majority of the last ten years struggling with the issue of my homosexuality, I do not expect anyone to understand my change in belief system, especially surrounding my sexual identity. What I do not understand is your fluctuating perception of what is right or wrong for my life.

## *What are the reasons for the Christian's condemnation of homosexuality?*

You said that you don't judge me for my "choices" and that your love for me as your brother is unwavering. I truly believe that, as I feel the same for you. And I know that your concern for my soul is based on what Fundamentalist Christianity says my fate is: that I am going to Hell because of what my sexual practices are. Believe me, this same belief has caused me much sorrow from the agonizing I have done over this message of hate. The intense discrimination and prejudice that I suffer every day from this message is a result, I believe, not from those who care for my well-being, but from those who are ignorant of the realities of being human and the interpretation of laws and commandments from scripture to people not of our time or culture. This has been illustrated throughout history toward many different races and culture. Not long ago, the church condoned slavery and the killing of Jews; beliefs that were supported by inaccurate interpretations of scripture. It is these same scriptures that people use today to condemn homosexuals.

## Does the Bible really condemn homosexuality?

I do not claim to be a Biblical scholar, but I do hold some theological background and education as you are well aware. Theologies of the world have always fascinated me and I have studied as many of them as I am able. There are three major portions of scripture that people use to condemn homosexuality. I believe them to be the basis for the Christian origin of homophobia, or the fear, hatred or lack of understanding of gays and lesbians. I would like to provide an opportunity for you to consider some alternative interpretations of these scriptures.

As we both know, translations of the Bible went through many hands and many minds before set to the words we read today. The Bible has also been passed down through many languages. As any interpreter will tell you (of which I am one) there are certain phrases or words that do not have an honest translation from one language to another. Interpreters merely do the best they can to convey what they feel to be the point. Again the teachings are open to new "interpretations." I do very much believe that the Bible is the inspired Word of God. Inspired by the Holy Spirit to men who were given a message to their contemporaries. It is not its validity or authenticity that I am questioning, only its interpretation by men who were not chosen to be the "inspired messengers." When comparing phrases of even a simple verse between two modern texts (The King James Version and the New International Version) we see a vast difference in meaning. The discrepancy of the words "debtors" and "trespassers" in The Lord's Prayer exemplifies this. Debtors, or persons that owe someone money or property, are clearly not the same as Trespassers, or persons who make unjustifiable claims on others. Both examples were translated by learned men, but which is correct? Which is most true to the original intent?

## *What are the scriptures Christians use to condemn homosexuality? What is an accurate contextual translation of them?*

The first passage of scripture that Christians use to condemn homosexuality is found in I Cor. 6:9-10. In the KJV, it states "Know ye not that the unrighteous shall not inherit the kingdom of God? Be not deceived: neither fornicators, nor idolaters, nor adulterers, nor effeminate, nor abusers of themselves with mankind, nor thieves, nor covetous, nor drunkards, nor revilers, nor extortionists, shall inherit the kingdom of God." (Most newer versions translate effeminate as male prostitutes or homosexual offenders.) If one considers the social climate of the Roman Empire and the full contextual lesson (of which this scripture is merely a short excerpt) then one can see why most contemporary theologians believe the lesson centers on mortal lusts and overmastered desires. No mention is made to persons whose true nature or natural sexual orientation is toward members of the same sex. In fact, the phrase homosexual offenders refers to people who are not gay, but practice homosexual acts, not homosexuals specifically. Historically, it was quite common and socially acceptable in that period for Roman men to "supplement" their marriage with a male prostitute or concubine. The subject therefore may be sex outside of marriage or extramarital affairs and the lust that drives these encounters.

The second passage is from the Israelite Holiness Code (a Jewish, not Christian belief system). In Leviticus Chapter 18, the code commands that men "shall not lie with a man as a woman." But in all fairness, those that continue to preach this very code today should also note the variety of violations they incur daily based on the selectively eliminated portions of the code. Consider your doomed fate when eating a rare steak, clam chowder or lobster (any meat with blood in it), or when sporting a new wool-cotton blend sweater (any garment made of two kinds of yarn), or when planting multiple crops on the same field. All these acts, (naming only a few items in the Israelite Holiness Code) are detestable things and everyone who does them will, according to this scripture, "be cut off from their people." Historically, the reasons given for these proscriptions were grounded in a desire for separation from other nations and their customs, avoidance of idolatry and a need for ceremonial cleanliness. The Jewish people of that time, which were commanded to follow this code, were small in number and were often in grave danger of being wiped out completely. The continuance of the family bloodlines and the culture as a whole was dependent upon male-female sexual intercourse. This alone, regardless of God's feelings on the subject, would proscribe an anti-gay mentality and law for a culture. All the instructions on sexual matters set forth in Leviticus promote survival of the culture and bloodline. Forbidden sexual acts include bestiality (which obviously does not create new children); incest (which contaminates the bloodline and can create genetic birth defects); fornication, or sex outside of marriage (which was not considered to provide a healthy environment for children born to the unwed mother) and sex with a woman during her menstrual period (which again is counter-productive to creating offspring). The Israelite Holiness Code (on the issue of sexual matters) states that sex is merely for reproduction so that the culture may survive. If we apply the restrictions of homosexual activity from this code to our lives today, then we must apply all of it. And that means no recreational sex.... period. How many Christians hold off having sex except for the purposes of procreation? How many Christians hold off having sex during the woman's menstrual cycle? How ridiculous it seems to me for Christians to condemn homosexuals based on this passage, especially when many break the code on a daily basis.

And lastly, the scripture most used and abused in favor of condemning the homosexual; the story of Sodom and Gomorrah. The story tells of two angels in the form of men sent to Sodom. Lot took them in and showed them hospitality, which was the custom. Then all the men of the city surrounded the house "both young and old; all the people from every quarter" and demanded to see the visitors. "Bring them out unto us, that we may know them." (Gen. 19:5 KJV) Know, of course, has been interpreted to mean many things. Some theologians believe that the men of Sodom wanted to meet and communicate with these powerful beings and became hostile only when Lot refused to allow it. Others would argue that know means intercourse or other sexual acts. Again, the original meaning is unclear after many centuries of interpretations. When Lot refused and begged the men to leave his guests alone (even offering his two virgin daughters instead), the men stormed the door and were struck blind by the angels. Lot and his family were told to flee the city, and Sodom was destroyed.

If "know" were truly meant to mean intercourse then I propose these considerations. The Bible is specific in saying that all the men of the city arrived at Lot's home without exception. The likelihood that the entire male population of Sodom was gay or even harbored homosexual tendencies is hardly viable, based on the common belief that approximately 10% of any given populace is gay or lesbian. More likely, assuming that the men meant intercourse, they were out for novelty and to humiliate the strangers. In that period, and even today, it is uncommon for male-male rape to be considered a sexual act. It is a method of showing power and control over another. (This is also true in male-female rape cases.) Some ancient cultures would flaunt their triumph over a conquered people by forcing captive men to take the part of the woman or be passive recipients to sexual intercourse. If this is the case, then Lot's offering of his daughters would mean nothing to the crowd. They were not out for sex, they were out to humiliate and conquer. Either way (and with either interpretation of the word know) the strangers were treated with contempt and not shown hospitality and kindness by the men of Sodom, which some theologians say was their greatest sin.

I was always taught that when looking at the Bible, if something is confusing, look further; the Bible will explain itself. It is its own best commentator. And in fact, there are several references to the doomed city in the Bible. Luke 10:10-13 states: "But into whatsoever city ye enter, and they receive you not...I say unto you, that it shall be more tolerable in that day (Judgment Day) for Sodom than for that city." Ezekiel 16:49-50 says: "This is the iniquity (great injustice) of your sister Sodom: pride, fullness of bread, and abundance of idleness was in her and in her daughters. Neither did she strengthen the hand of the poor and needy. And they were haughty, and committed abomination before me: therefore

I took them away as I saw good." Despite the assumptions of some theologians that abomination refers to homosexual acts, they are not specifically mentioned. Instead, this passage (in its entirety) specifically mentions greed, rebellion against God, empty rituals, failure to plead the cause of orphans and widows, failure to pursue justice, and failure to champion the oppressed. No mention of homosexuality is made. Jude 7 makes the only reference to the sexual nature of the citizens of Sodom. "Even as Sodom and Gomorrah...giving themselves over to fornication (heterosexual intercourse outside of marriage) and going after strange flesh." The Jerusalem Bible footnotes this scripture with "they lusted not after human beings, but after the strangers who were angels, Gen. 19:1-11." Once again, homosexuality is not mentioned in the text of the Bible, only assumed in the interpretations of certain theologians.

## *How can scripture support homosexuality and gay relationships?*

There are also many issues relating to gays and lesbians that are not even approached in the Bible. The Bible makes no reference to lesbians or lesbian acts. Would this lead one to believe that same sex relations between women are acceptable, whereas same sex relations between men are not? Here again we are looking at text set forth by a cultural interpretation of God's Word. This belief has been true in many cultures throughout history. Women in love (or even women in general) are considered weak and submissive. If two men enter into a relationship, then "one or both must be weak or passive." The concept of men in love distorts the Patriarchal belief system that Men are more powerful and dominant over Women. These notions (incorrect as I believe them to be) threaten to destroy the very foundation of male-driven cultures like those cited in the Bible.

The Bible also makes no mention of long-term gay or lesbian relationships/marriage. They are quite common and have been for centuries, yet only the sexual act itself is mentioned. And even it is only mentioned clearly and without question in the Israelite Holiness Code. Most references to condemned sexual acts in the Bible and in sermons use the phrase "unnatural acts." To this I give my heaviest argument; one that I know we may never agree on. God created me the way I am. I stand average in height. My eyes are hazel and my hair brown. I have my Father's eyes, my Grandpa's nose, my mother's mouth and my Grandma's cheekbones. I have an aptitude for music and performing arts. I am gay. We are all the results of random acts of chromosomal union, chance and (if God made all these other things, then) God, too. I did not choose to be gay. I was born gay. I know no one who would joyously state that they would want to be born into a minority that is so disdained by some segments of society that they are considered worse than serial killers and should be put to instant and painful death. My gay-ness is natural; as natural as breathing. It would be unnatural for me to engage in sexual relations with a woman and therefore, I believe, abhorrent is God's eyes. The only choice that I made in this matter was the choice to be true to God, myself and others. That sense of integrity, hard won as it has been, has given me great personal pride. And no one will take it from me.

## *What should be our response to these judgments?*
If I suffer from any illness, mental or physical, it is a result of my environment as a child, which forbade me to learn, discuss or explore my sexual identity. We are all innately very sexual beings, and to deny the realization of our sensuality is to stunt a crucial part of our development. I may not have opened the door into my gayness until later than most, but that is not because it wasn't there to open. Fear, guilt and abhorrence of homosexuality kept the doors tightly boarded until those

influences were far from my consciousness. I have spent the majority of my adult life fighting and giving in to my sexual urges with many men whose first names I didn't even know. And finally I have met someone who I want to spend my life with in a committed, safe and fulfilling relationship. But I can't share this happiness with any of my family because in your eyes I am an abomination to God, and if you don't believe that, then you should be able to accept my sexuality as natural and good. You can't just turn your heads and cry out to God in prayer over my lost soul.

I believe that the Bible is one of the most important texts in the history of mankind. But more important still is the examination of cultural interpretations of it. Passing through so many hands, open to so many interpretations, the Bible, in the hands of learned (but not necessarily righteous) men, has been used to support many destructive personal and social ideologies. The Bible was used to justify the Holy Crusades which wiped out hundreds of thousands of undesirables in Northern Africa, Southern Europe and Asia. Slave owners of the South (and even white supremacists today) used the Bible to support their beliefs in racial purity and self empowerment over other human beings. Hitler was an avid reader of the Bible and supporter of the church. These teachers, who cited scripture to support their personal agendas, had large numbers of unquestioning followers. These teachers were believed to be right and holy men. I don't think today's society or contemporary theologians would find scriptural support for their actions, but these right and holy men swore it was there. Were they misguided? Are we?

It all basically comes down to the fact that we believe what we will. And sometimes we will hold to our ideals so tightly, so terrified that an inkling of doubt or new information will destroy our entire belief structure, that we close out the opportunity to reexamine and strengthen our beliefs. Every so often these structures, much like a home, must be given a good once over. I had to give mine a thorough inspection because I was unable to live in it anymore. It was too filled with guilt, sorrow and misery. That is not something that the Lord created for me. He created my life to be filled with happiness and righteousness.

You had mentioned to me on the phone that you were not scholarly enough to defend yourself against my arguments. My charge to you is: seek understanding. If you are passionate enough about what you believe, and not just accepting of what your minister preaches at church, then you will look for some answers. I don't expect this letter to change any of your beliefs. I only hope that I have given you an opportunity to understand some of mine. When push comes to shove on the subject of God and religion, it comes down to the fact that none of us will fully understand all of this until we come face to face with our maker. When that time comes, I feel that I will be able to face God with what really matters; a clean heart, mind and soul. And I think that God will be proud of me and the way I have treated my fellow human.

The book that I mentioned to you on the phone is called "Is the Homosexual My Neighbor? Another Christian View" by Scanzoni and Mollenkott. I am using it for some research so I can't send it at this time, but I hope you will want to get it for yourself. I want you to know that I adore you as my sister, and will always respect and admire you. That is all I ask in return. Please write when you can, I know this is a lot to digest.

(Since this letter was written almost 10 years ago, my relationship with my sister has greatly improved. Whenever she visits from out of town she stays in our home and has become great friends with my partner. I really believe that our commitment to staying connected has led to a transformed relationship. While some family members may never react positively to your relationship, try to keep the door open for dialogue. You don't have to compromise who you are to stay connected to family. We will explore more of this in Session 5.)

## *Making Christ Our Mediator*

Resolving the conflicts that religious oppression creates begins by repairing its damage to our relationships. While many gays and lesbians left the church because of oppression, discrimination and ostracism, evidence of a new "welcoming church" is growing through mainstream religion. One publication, "Open Hands," was begun several decades ago by the United Methodist-affiliated Reconciling Congregation Program in Chicago. Its efforts include seeking the elimination of same-sex discrimination and encouraging diversity throughout its congregations. Presently, almost 500 welcoming churches are part of the organization.[23] Awareness and understanding that "God did not put us here to damn us" is the first step toward healing and acceptance.[24] "There is nothing," Dr. Richard A. Isay maintains, "like the power of being loved over a long period of time. We can undo the sense of being unloved and unlovable by tapping into the healing process of our relationships."[25]

Dedicated efforts in the United Church of Christ since 1983 have created a powerful alliance and support system for LGBT Christians. The UCC Coalition for LGBT Concerns' mission is to: provide support and sanctuary to all lesbian, gay, bisexual and transgender sisters and brothers, their families and friends; advocate for their full inclusion in church and society; and bring Christ's affirming message of love and justice for all people. The United Church of Christ Coalition for Lesbian, Gay, Bisexual, and Transgender Concerns is officially recognized by the United Church of Christ as a related, self-created organization. The Coalition's work includes:

- Creating and supporting Open and Affirming (ONA) settings within the United Church of Christ

- Supporting youth and young adults and those who work with them

23. Hoffman.
24. Jucha.
25. Peterson.

- Local organizing and outreach. The Coalition's ministry is rooted in working for peace and justice, inspired by the Good News of God's extravagant welcome.

www.ucccoalition.org

**What are some Christ-centered solutions for our relationship disputes?**

# How can we make Christ a part of our relationship?

_____

_____

_____

_____

_____

_____

_____

_____

How can we make the church a part of our lives together as
a gay couple?

_____

_____

_____

_____

_____

_____

_____

_____

# Session #2 - Homophobia in Society and in Ourselves

## *Homophobia in Society*

Our discussion begins by exploring the external force of homophobia, its roots in a heterosexual society, and its subsequent internalization in homosexual relationships. Homophobia can be considered a result of society's repulsion to homosexuality. These anti-homosexual attitudes arouse disabling anxieties in homosexual individuals and make it difficult for them to sustain lasting emotional commitments.[26] This homophobia develops because society's view of "family" is threatened by the idea of a homosexual relationship.

**How have I been affected by homophobia in society?**

_____

_____

_____

_____

_____

---

26. Alan Bell, Martin Weinberg, and Sue Kiefer Hammersmith, *Sexual Preference: Its Development in Men and Women* (Bloomington: Indiana UP, 1988), p. 83.

Not being able to show affection in public or dealing with disapproval from the family are ways in which homosexual relationship issues differ.[27] In heterosexual couples "families help buffer conflicts with couples by taking the marriage seriously, giving financial assistance, and providing emotional support. But many parents have a hard time extending this same acknowledgment to gay relationships."[28]

## How does external homophobia affect our relationship?

27. Betty Berzon, *Permanent Partners: Building Gay & Lesbian Relationships That Last* (NY: Dutton, 2004), p. 17.
28. Rik Isensee, *Love Between Men: Enhancing Intimacy and Keeping Your Relationship Alive* (NY: Prentice Hall, 1992), p. 119.

# *Homophobia in Ourselves*
## What is internalized homophobia?

Homophobia in our society creates internal stressors for homosexual couples. One such stressor is the development of a negative gay identity. Acknowledging one's gayness often involves a struggle to define who you are outside a sexual connotation. Betty Berzon suggests that the development of a positive gay identity involves a struggle to integrate something that many believe to be discrediting. Gays and lesbians are forced to accept their sexuality in a context of confusion and self-deprecation. She believes that these internal feelings exist in the "unconscious mind" and have a specific effect on the "quality of our adult gay and lesbian sexual relationships."[29]

A perception exists in gay men particularly that homosexuality denotes a failure to achieve a masculine sexual adjustment.[30] These identity issues have been responsible for increased feelings of internalized homophobia in the gay community. Kirstin A. Hancock summarizes an analysis of this development by researchers in the field. These feelings involve the "incorporation of anti-gay prejudice into the self-image of a lesbian or gay individual." This process begins after homosexual children become aware that they are different. As they mature into adults they associate their differences with society's negative attitudes, eventually incorporating a negative self-image resulting in varying degrees of internalized homophobia. These feelings may range from "a mild tendency toward self-doubt in the face of prejudice to overt self-hatred to self-destructive behavior."[31] Dr. Isay believes that our society creates problems for gays and lesbians entering into relationships. When society rejects their relationships, the resulting rage is often internalized. A positive gay identity is crucial before a relationship can successfully develop.[32]

29. Berzon, p. 17.
30. Bell, p. 127.
31. Kirstin A. Hancock, "Psychotherapy with Lesbians and Gay Men," *Lesbian, Gay, and Bisexual Identities Over the Lifespan: Psychological Perspectives*, Anthony R. D'Augelli and Charlotte Patterson, eds. (Oxford: Oxford UP, 1995), p. 400.
32. Andrea L. T. Peterson, "Dr. Richard Discusses the Value and Difficulties of Gay Relationships," *Dallas Voice*, 14 Jun. 1996.

Describe your identity as a gay or lesbian person.
In what kind of situations do you feel positive?

_____

_____

_____

_____

_____

_____

In what kind of situations do you feel negative?

_____

_____

_____

_____

_____

_____

**How does internalized homophobia affect relationships?**
Because society is so hesitant to accept the homosexual's lifestyle, gay and lesbian relationships have no legitimacy in the heterosexual world. This illegitimacy is evident by the lack of social support for homosexual relationships. John H. Driggs and Steven E. Finn argue that this lack of support encourages "isolation and secrecy,"[33] which makes the relationship more at risk.[34] Society's stigma of homosexuality prevents many gay and lesbian couples from being open about their relationships.[35] This stigma comes from a belief that the homosexual's life style isn't successful because of its transitory and underground elements.[36] The results are tormented couples who isolate their relationships rather than disclose them to a homophobic society.

One step from legitimacy is legality. The contracts and legal ties of marriage have been shown to serve as barriers to leaving a relationship for heterosexual couples.[37] The absence of legally sanctioning a homosexual union adds to their temporary nature and probably accounts for their relative instability.[38] After considering the absence of insurance benefits, tax breaks, spousal discounts, and other practical rewards for homosexual couples, we are reminded of "society's view of same-sex liaisons as transitory, illicit, and not to be taken seriously. Unfortunately, too often these attitudes become internalized and thus plague the lovers' relationship from within."[39]

33. John H. Driggs and Steven E. Finn, *Intimacy Between Men* (NY: Dutton-Penguin, 1991), p. 136.
34. Berzon, p. 16.
35. Hancock, p. 408.
36. Berzon, p. 10.
37. Hancock, p. 408.
38. Bell, p. 83, 102.
39. Berzon, p. 16.

# How does internalized homophobia affect our relationship?

## *Strategies To Combat Homophobia*
### Developing a Positive Gay Identity by Establishing Legitimacy in Our Relationships

Although society is evolving toward legitimizing homosexual relationships, gays and lesbians can develop effective strategies for dealing with homophobia in society and in their families. A study accomplished by the California School of Professional Psychology at Almeda found that the evidence of social support for gay and lesbian couples was predictive of relationship quality. This support came from friends more so than family. More support was perceived by couples who had higher relationship satisfaction.[40] Dr. Tina Tessina suggests that couples must seek approval of their relationships so that their commitments in turn will be healthier and happier.[41]

### Integrating into the Gay Community

Additionally, because the gay community is becoming more supportive and nurturing of gay couples, integrating into it will encourage better support for the relationship. J. Harry and R. Lovely studied relationships of over 200 gay persons and found that those who were integrated into the gay community were more satisfied with their relationships and had more intimate emotional experiences.[42] Although a perception exists that the "gay bar" is just a place for sexual exploration, many researchers conclude that it is the "principal meeting place for friends, a place of refuge from heterosexual society, and a communications center where people can keep up with what is going on in the gay world...and therefore a place serving more of a social than sexual purpose."[43]

---

40. George M. Cuesta-Aragon, "The Effect of Knowledge of Human Immunodeficiency Virus Infection on the Quality of Gay Male Relationships," (www.gay.net, 30 Mar. 1997)
41. Tina Tessina, *Gay Relationships* (NY: Putnam, 1990), p. 26.
42. Driggs, p. 134.
43. Bell, p. 180.

# How are we integrated into the gay community?

_____

_____

_____

_____

_____

_____

_____

_____

## Guidelines for "Coming Out"

An important step for legitimizing one's relationship and dissolving feelings of internalized homophobia is through a process known as "coming out." Isay believes that gay couples would do well "to come out as much as possible. When we come out our social and intimate relationships are better. We function better in many areas. Some even say that once they have come out they can even think more clearly."[44] Tessina feels that "making the decision to come out...is a profound life decision, and anyone who makes it is moved to reflect on a philosophy of life. Like all rites of passage, it is a hard-won experience."[45] Rik Isensee knows the significance of coming out to families for most gay men. "We may have thought about disclosing our sexual orientation for a long time, hoping parents would appreciate our desire to include them in our lives. Revealing such an intimate aspect of ourselves is an attempt to let our families know who we really are, so our future relationships can be more genuine."[46] Strategies for "coming out" will be presented in Session #5.

44. Peterson.
45. Tessina, p. 24.
46. Isensee, p. 113.

YOU ARE NOT THE LABELS THAT
HAVE BEEN PLACED ON YOU.
(you are not the labels that
you have placed on you.)

Allow the labels to fall away
and reveal your
spirit. you can
be all things
in the present
moment. There
are no more
limits.

# Session #3 - Sex Roles and Socialization

## *The Battle of the Same-Sexes*

Because there are few homosexual role models for gay and lesbians to observe, issues often "taken for granted" in heterosexual relationships must be discussed and negotiated. For instance, the decision to combine incomes and property or choosing one's career over another may increase the probability of conflict in the relationship.[47] The lack of positive role models for gay couples contributes significantly to the confusion over sex-roles. Couples rely on heterosexual role models they have learned through socialization and conditioning.

Yet for gay men, this conditioning or socialization can interfere with the development of a committed relationship. Since their socialization consists of conforming to analytical or critical stereotypes, gay men in relationships tend to be more focused on their own independence. What results is a lack of attention to the partner's emotional needs and an escalation of conflict over "who is right" instead of "how they feel."

Isensee believes that "by understanding how we've been conditioned by these roles, we can balance traditional male abilities with skills associated with female sex roles: disclosing our feelings, listening to our partner, and developing an intuitive

---

47. John H. Driggs and Steven E. Finn, *Intimacy Between Men* (NY: Dutton-Penguin, 1991), p. 131.

sense for the emotional needs of our relationship." Men are taught not to express emotional vulnerability. We rationalize our feelings by telling ourselves there's no reason to feel sad, hurt or insecure. Since men are not socialized to "settle down", there is an expectation not to do so.[48]

**What are some sex role issues in your relationship that may be a result of socialization in society?**

48. Rik Isensee, *Love Between Men: Enhancing Intimacy and Keeping Your Relationship Alive* (NY: Prentice Hall, 1992), pp. 5, 23, 94.

Another important issue involves the existence of intra-gender empathy and intra-gender identity. Having a partner with like tastes and desires can cause relationship isolation and sexual boredom. Even though gays and lesbians are more in touch with their partner's sexual needs, this familiarity could be cause for the couple to eventually view sex as predictable and unfulfilling.[49] In addition, Isay notes that gay men so often say they want someone like themselves in terms of education, social standing, age, religion or geographical background. He says that these similarities do not sustain excitement in the relationship. Rather, differences are very important to maintaining passion in relationships. It is therefore vital for couples to explore their differences.[50] Hancock also suggests that gay men tend to resemble one another in their relationships. "Gender-role socialization trains men to separate sex from love, to be dominant, sexually active, and reluctant to express emotion, which inhibits the development of intimacy." She asserts that when two men become sexually involved, these characteristics become pronounced.[51] Berzon believes that homosexual couples must contend with many issues that are structured by gender-role expectations. Often the smallest issues concerning who will do the cooking, cleaning or managing the money can become "arduous and cumbersome."[52]

49. Driggs, pp. 136, 156.
50. Andrea L. T. Peterson, "Dr. Richard Discusses the Value and Difficulties of Gay Relationships," *Dallas Voice*, 14 Jun. 1996.
51. Kirstin A. Hancock, "Psychotherapy with Lesbians and Gay Men," *Lesbian, Gay, and Bisexual Identities Over the Lifespan: Psychological Perspectives*, Anthony R. D'Augelli and Charlotte Patterson, eds. (Oxford: Oxford UP, 1995), p. 408.
52. Betty Berzon, *Permanent Partners: Building Gay & Lesbian Relationships That Last* (NY: Dutton, 2004), p. 18.

## What are your similarities as a couple?

_____

_____

_____

_____

_____

_____

## What are your differences?

_____

_____

_____

_____

_____

_____

_____

_____

Some sex-role related conflicts in homosexual relationships can be typical of heterosexual couples. Concurrent problems include money, career choices, and competition. However, in a gay relationship, the competition may be more narrowly defined. Attractiveness, salaries, education, friends, physical strength, or other ways of balancing power and status are more common to gay male couples. The competitiveness between gay men may not surface until the couple begins seeking interactions outside the relationship. Isensee notes that in its initial stage, the relationship is the center of a couple's interaction. Later other interactions, such as career, friendships and the larger community, threaten this exclusivity. In an effort to resolve conflicts associated with competitiveness, the gay couple may isolate themselves from their community and look to the relationship "to satisfy all of their desires for honest human contact."[53]

## How have you experienced competition in your relationship?

53. Isensee, p. 125.

This kind of isolation creates pseudo-intimacy between partners. The illusion that intimacy exists is validated when couples become so interdependent that they lose their identities as individuals. When couples spend all of their time together, it can "discourage individual risk taking and block personal growth." Psycho-therapeutic identification of pseudo-intimacy includes "dependency," "co-dependency," "enmeshment," or "relationship addiction."[54] Lesbian couples tend to face fears of losing their mates. This propels some partners into being overly involved in the relationship. Sometimes they become so involved that they lose a sense of themselves to the greater good of the relationship.[55]

**How have you experienced co-dependency in your relationships?**

_____

_____

_____

_____

_____

_____

_____

_____

_____

_____

54. Driggs, pp. 15, 135-136.
55. Uneeda White, "Therapists Discuss Finding a Balance in Lesbian and Gay Unions," _Dallas Voice_, 28 Feb. 1997.

## *Learning to be Different*

Isensee believes it is helpful to establish some independence as a means of avoiding relationship isolation. Since men are socialized to function independently, a male couple may have a difficult time finding the balance of "who I am, who are you, and who are we together."[56] Tessina notes that "lesbian couples should work to create space between themselves, clearly outline financial jobs, work toward a positive view of self, assign parenting guidelines, and seek ways to spark romance and sexual activity."[57] She believes that developing better communication and negotiation techniques will improve relationship dynamics. [58]

**How can you develop independence in your relationship?**

_____

_____

_____

_____

_____

_____

Isensee encourages the development of listening skills. He says that, "Men often argue about ideas, rather than talking about feelings. Disputing ideas can inhibit your awareness of what's really at stake for you. When you look for logical contradictions in order to counter each other's feelings, you're not really listening. This is a "logical" mistake, if you will--emotions don't generally respond to logic. Feelings simply press for recognition,

56. Isensee, p. 8.
57. Tessina, p. 23.
58. Ibid., p. 86.

and often shift as soon as they're acknowledged. Understanding doesn't equal agreement, but accurate listening helps you understand each other's point of view, so you can clearly state what your conflict is about. You may still need to work on solving it, but your ability to find a mutually acceptable solution will be greatly improved by clarifying your differences. A defensive response is basically an attempt to get your partner to stop feeling, so you won't feel blamed.[59]

**What are some "good listening" techniques?**

 

 

 

 

 

**What are some healthy ways you communicate with your partner?**

 

 

 

 

59. Isensee, pp. 10-11.

## *Being a Role Model for the Others*

What are some ways we can be role models for the gay community?

<br><br><br><br><br><br>

What can we learn from Christ concerning role modeling?

<br><br><br><br><br><br><br><br>

# Session #4 - Promiscuity In Gay Relationships

## *Examining Sexual Freedom*
**Why is promiscuity so prevalent in the gay community?  Is it right or wrong?**

Promiscuity is a force by which real intimacy between couples can become illusive. Promiscuity in gay relationships is a result of a "greater tendency of males in general to separate sex from affection, to estimate their personal worth on the basis of how much sex they have, and to view fidelity as an undesirable restriction upon their freedom and independence." Bell and Weinberg believe that this is because few alternatives exist where gay men can meet on anything more than a sexual basis. They contend that, "Driven underground, segregated in what have been termed 'sexual marketplaces,' threatened but perhaps also stimulated by the danger of their enterprise, homosexual men would be expected to have an enormous number of fleeting sexual encounters.  Sex with persons other than strangers can, in fact, be a liability, the occasion for blackmail and unwanted public exposure. In other words, sex without commitment or much involvement may reflect an even greater commitment to the reality of their circumstances, given the 'homoerotophobic' society in which they live."[60]

---

60.  Alan Bell, Martin Weinberg, and Sue Kiefer Hammersmith, *Sexual Preference: Its Development in Men and Women* (Bloomington: Indiana UP, 1988), p. 101.

## Does promiscuity threaten the success of long-term gay relationships?

The absence of monogamy in gay relationships has also been documented by other researchers. Driggs and Finn noted that 82 percent of gay men, in a study conducted by Blumstein and Schwartz, were sexually active outside their partnerships. In fact, the longer the relationship lasted, the less sexual exclusivity was present. Additionally, McWhirter and Mattison found that 95 percent of the couples in their study were not monogamous. All of the couples in their survey who had been together longer than five years were having sexual relations with other men. They suggest that "although many gay men are raised to believe that sexual exclusivity is a matter of morality, they come to regard this as a matter of traditional heterosexual values. This stance makes it easier (for them) to explore nontraditional arrangements in their relationships."[61]

## What causes gay partners to become promiscuous?

Dr. Mel O. Karmen, a counselor for homosexual couples in San Diego, believes that boredom in a gay relationship is the primary cause for promiscuity.[62] Edmond White maintains that promiscuity has been an integral part of the gay culture. In a community primarily composed of gay bars, bath houses and nightclubs, the tendency to be inundated with opportunities to have sex perpetuate non-monogamy. The difference between gays and lesbians is the culture in which their relationships thrive. Lesbians can meet each other at feminist rallies or during other activities exclusive to women.[63] Even with the acceptance of promiscuity, 85 percent of gay male couples had their greatest conflicts over outside relationships. Being promiscuous while in a relationship "replaces or interferes with sex between partners... [and] discourages gay couples from confronting deeper issues of anger, distrust, or jealousy that might otherwise arise."[64]

61. Ibid., p. 151.
62. Uneeda White, "Therapists Discuss Finding a Balance in Lesbian and Gay Unions," *Dallas Voice*, 28 Feb. 1997.
63. Edmund White, *States of Desire: Travels in Gay America* (NY: Penguin, 1991), p. xiv.
64. John H. Driggs and Steven E. Finn, *Intimacy Between Men* (NY: Dutton-Penguin, 1991), p. 155.

## Is there a difference between promiscuity and infidelity?

On the question of fidelity, Isensee relates that unlike heterosexual relationships where infidelity may indicate "distress between the partners," gay men do not view sexual contact outside the relationship as a violation of the commitment. What it does create is an unproductive avenue for abdicating one's responsibility to "building an emotionally fulfilling relationship" and enabling an environment for confronting future conflict.[65] Blumstein and Schwartz conclude that "gay male couples who were monogamous in their first two years together were more likely to stay together than couples who were not monogamous. After the first two years, monogamy was unrelated to the persistence of a relationship."[66] Berzon echoes these sentiments. She believes that "what works best in enduring relationships is monogamy. For gay men, outside sex has really been an escape hatch that gets used when there are difficult things to deal with in the relationship. It's just much easier to go outside the primary partnership where there's always a challenge and excitement and so on."[67]

## How do you feel about sexual encounters outside the relationship?

65. Rik Isensee, *Love Between Men: Enhancing Intimacy and Keeping Your Relationship Alive* (NY: Prentice Hall, 1992), p. 94.
66. Driggs, p. 152.
67. Daniel Vaillancourt, "Berzon Counsels Couples for the Long Haul with The Intimacy Dance," *Dallas Voice*, 23 Aug. 1996.

## *Monogamy Vs. Open Relationships*
**What are the pros and cons of having a monogamous relationship?**

Berzon believes that establishing permanence in homosexual unions should be goals for all gays and lesbians. "Though the timeline may vary for couples, a long-term relationship is one that assumes permanence and that has endured enough time for the partners to have shared formulative experiences."[68] Isay also calls all gay and lesbian couples to work toward commitment. "Too often the excitement wears off too quickly. We don't put in the effort to maintain...both the commitment and the passion within the primary relationship. But the partner has to be of primary emotional importance if a sexually non monogamous relationship is to work."[69]

**What do you feel about monogamy?**

_____

_____

_____

_____

_____

_____

_____

_____

68. Elizabeth Wallace, "Berzon Hopes to Help Couples Commit For Life," *Washington Blade*, 22 Nov. 1996.
69. Andrea L. T. Peterson, "Dr. Richard Discusses the Value and Difficulties of Gay Relationships," *Dallas Voice*, 14 Jun. 1996.

### What are the pros and cons of having an open relationship?

Sometimes monogamy is not a desire for couples. Although some research suggests that couples with "open" relationships do worry more about their relationship lasting,[70] Isensee suggest that "looking at what we hope either monogamy or non-monogamy would resolve in our relationships can help us identify what's really at the heart of this conflict."[71] When choosing a relationship that is open to outside sexual partners, consider some ground rules. These ground rules should be clear about what each partner wants so that there is no confusion about what is allowed. Berzon believes that "these ground rules [must] really come from what you want, not what you think you should be saying. And then, be consistent. Or at least be willing to keep talking about how it's going."[72]

### What are ground rules for an open relationship?

_____

_____

_____

_____

_____

_____

_____

_____

_____

_____

_____

70. Alan Bell, Martin Weinberg, and Sue Kiefer Hammersmith, _Sexual Preference: Its Development in Men and Women_ (Bloomington: Indiana UP, 1988), p. 133.
71. Isensee, p. 93.
72. Vaillancourt.

# *Establishing a Faithful Commitment*
## How can we make monogamy work for us?

Many organizations exist to make this commitment easier.
The National Gay and Lesbian Task Force (NGLTF) recently
released the publication "To Have and To Hold: Organizing for
Marriage." This document helps couples prepare for commitment
ceremonies while advocating homosexuals' freedom to marry.[73]
The NGLTF believes that the fight for the freedom to marry
for gays must begin at the grassroots level. Two such groups,
the Hawaii Equal Rights Marriage Project (HERMP) and the Na
Mamo O Hawaii (NMOH), serve to effect change in the state
legislature. These and other organizations are important for
legitimizing gay and lesbian marriages.

**What are the local organizations in our state working for marriage equality?**

_____

_____

_____

_____

_____

_____

_____

73. National Gay and Lesbian Task Force, "Get the NGLTF Action Kit on Same-Sex Marriages," www.gay.net (30 Mar. 1997).

love is for...giving

# Session #5 - Biological Family and "Families Of Choice"

## *The Biological Conflict*

In many gay and lesbian relationships couples are often still in the closet from their families. Most counselors agree that this is a unique problem for homosexual relationships. Isensee suggests that for heterosexual couples, "Families help buffer conflicts with couples by taking the marriage seriously, giving financial assistance, and providing emotional support. But many parents have a hard time extending this same acknowledgment to gay relationships."[74] What results is a relationship that may not have anywhere to go for support and advice.

**Does my family know about my sexual orientation? What is my response to them?**

_____

_____

_____

_____

_____

74. Rik Isensee, *Love Between Men: Enhancing Intimacy and Keeping Your Relationship Alive* (NY: Prentice Hall, 1992), p. 119.

The absence of legitimacy for homosexual relationships by society adds significant additional stressors for couples. Driggs and Finn argue that this lack of support encourages "isolation and secrecy." If you cannot hold hands without others threatening you, you will not feel comfortable together. If it is not safe to identify yourselves in public as a couple, you will stay at home. And unless you know other people with whom you can be open, you will not invite others into your home because it is awkward to explain who your lover is. Social disapproval of gay and lesbian couples is probably the primary cause of relationship isolation.[75]

Dr. Lawrence Kurdek asserts that "societal stigma against homosexuality prevents many gay and lesbian couples from being open about their relationships. There is also far less social and familial support for gay and lesbian couples than for heterosexual."[76] This stigma comes from a belief that the homosexual's life style wasn't successful because of the transitory and underground elements.[77] Gay men and lesbian women lived dual lives, fearing their discovery would be worse than the anguish of hiding one's true self.

75.  John H. Driggs and Steven E. Finn, Intimacy Between Men (NY: Dutton-Penguin, 1991), p. 136.
76.  Kirstin A. Hancock, "Psychotherapy with Lesbians and Gay Men," *Lesbian, Gay, and Bisexual Identities Over the Lifespan: Psychological Perspectives*, Anthony R. D'Augelli and Charlotte Patterson, eds. (Oxford: Oxford UP, 1995), p. 408.
77.  Betty Berzon, *Permanent Partners: Building Gay & Lesbian Relationships That Last* (NY: Dutton, 2004), p. 10.

**Do I hide my sexual relationship from my family? What is their response to my partner?**

One step from legitimacy is legality. Hancock cites that the contracts and legal ties of marriage have been shown to serve as barriers to leaving a relationship.[78] Bell and Weinberg agree that the absence of legally sanctioning a homosexual union adds to their temporary nature and probably accounts for their relative instability.[79] After considering the absence of the benefits of marriage, such as; insurance benefits, tax breaks, spousal discounts, and other practical rewards, we are reminded of "society's view of same-sex liaisons as transitory, illicit, and not to be taken seriously. Unfortunately, too often these attitudes become internalized and thus plague the lovers' relationship

78. Hancock.
79. Alan Bell, Martin Weinberg, and Sue Kiefer Hammersmith, *Sexual Preference: Its Development in Men and Women* (Bloomington: Indiana UP, 1988), pp. 83, 102.

from within."[80] Because of the issues constantly facing gay and lesbian couples, strains can develop especially when your family pretends he/she doesn't exist, or denies the significance of your relationship.

## How does my relationship with family affect the relationship with my partner?

_____

_____

_____

_____

_____

_____

## Should I "come out" to my family? And if so, how should I do it?

Isensee knows the significance of coming out to families for most gay men. "We may have thought about disclosing our sexual orientation for a long time, hoping parents would appreciate our desire to include them in our lives. Revealing such an intimate aspect of ourselves is an attempt to let our families know who we really are, so our future relationships can be more genuine."[81] He sets some guidelines for gay men looking to come out to family:

80. Berzon, p. 16.
81. Isensee, p. 113.

1) Come out when you're feeling good about yourself--not when you are feeling emotionally vulnerable, they may have such a deep emotional response to your disclosure that they won't be able to help you sort through your feelings;

2) Have a support system--anyone you feel close to who will be available before, during, and after your disclosure;

3) Listen and reflect--don't counter their objections or educate them about their prejudices. Let them go through their own process as parents of a gay son or daughter;

4) Limit your interaction--you're probably not the best person to help them process their feelings. After you have reflected their concerns and affirmed your desire for continued contact, they may be willing to reach out to PFLAG;

5) Don't retaliate--they may take out their disappointment on you. If you can simply hear that they're upset and avoid retaliating, you may be able to keep the conflict from escalating. It may have taken years for you to come to terms with it, they may need as much time also;

6) Keep channels of communication open--write or telephone when you feel calmer, listen to them and reflect their feelings, acknowledge their disappointment and underlying concern, let them know that the reason you decided to tell them was that you wanted to feel closer, and stress your desire for continued contact.[82]

82. Ibid., pp. 114-116.

To whom do you want (or need) to come out? Why?

_____

_____

_____

_____

_____

_____

_____

_____

## *Families of Choice*
### What if I'm not ready to come out to my family or they don't accept me?

Because the gay community is becoming more supportive and nurturing of gay couples, integrating into it will encourage better support for the relationship. J. Harry and R. Lovely studied relationships of over 200 men and found that those who were integrated into the gay community were more satisfied with their relationships and had more intimate emotional experiences.[83]

A commonality in heterosexual and homosexual relationships is the occasional reoccurrence of ex-lovers. Paul Smith, a clinical social worker who primarily counsels gay men, says, "When there is a breakup, I think one of the things people dread most is running into the person [they used to date]," Smith said. "The second most dreaded thing is running into the partner with someone else, who the person who has been left often sees as their replacement. Some former couples get accustomed to the idea, but others continue to have a problem. ... It's harder if one is dating, and the other is not."[84]

And the issues are the same for lesbians.

"In heterosexual relationships, guys have their friends and girls have their friends, so when you break up you both go your separate ways and you have your friends," she said. "But in lesbian relationships, your friends are her friends and her friends are your friends. There's no separate group to go to; it's just one big circle."[85]

83. Driggs, p. 134.
84. Sue Fox, "The Ex-Files: When the Lovin' Ends, the Drama Begins," *Washington Blade*, 9 Aug. 1996.
85. Ibid.

**Develop a sense of family with each other and avoiding premature commitment.**

Kurdek cites a report by McWhirter and Mattison in which most of the male couples they studied moved in together after about one month of acquaintance while M. Nichols commented on the relatively short courtship period for lesbians.[86] In searching for ways to make their relationship work, some gays and lesbians jump into commitment and monogamy too quickly or adopt inflexible rules that inhibit personal growth within the relationship. Others go to the other extreme and, feeling lost without social rules, fall into self-destructive relationships. Without the security of knowing what will work, homosexual men and women often have trouble in evaluating the possibilities before making a commitment. In essence, they follow no rules, and as a result they can become confused, hurt, and lost. They may become involved in one destructive relationship after another, engage in promiscuous sex without satisfaction or goals, or simply jump into relationships without first dating to become acquainted with the other person. Often, because they feel that relationships won't work anyway, gay people avoid commitment and intimacy altogether and become lonely and isolated.[87]

Berzon believes that a lack of role models with which to "design our own relationships" causes gays and lesbians to "scrap a relationship rather than work through the problems."[88] Often homosexuals, in an attempt to find a relationship that will legitimize their own identity, enter into commitments prematurely.

---

86. Lawrence Kurdek, "Lesbian and Gay Couples," *Lesbian, Gay, and Bisexual Identities Over the Lifespan: Psychological Perspectives*, Anthony R. D'Augelli and Charlotte Patterson, eds. (Oxford: Oxford UP, 1995), p. 245.
87. Tina Tessina, *Gay Relationships* (NY: Putnam, 1990), p. 13.
88. Elizabeth Wallace, "Berzon Hopes to Help Couples Commit For Life," *Washington Blade*, 22 Nov. 1996.

# What is our commitment between us?

_____

_____

_____

_____

_____

_____

_____

_____

_____

_____

## Understand the differences in gay relationships.

Isensee notes that in its initial stage, the relationship is the center of a couple's interaction. Later other interactions, such as career, friendships and the larger community threaten this exclusivity. In heterosexual society, the relationship served a "social function." "[F]amily life served as a link to the rest of the community, and was in turn nurtured and supported by common rituals and rites of passage, such as marriage, having kids, and funerals." However in gay life together, non-acceptance of the relationship intensified by discrimination and prejudice can lead to extreme isolation. The gay couple in turn looks to the relationship "to satisfy all of their desires for honest human contact." Dr. George F. Solomon, in a psychoneuroimmunilogy assessment of persons with AIDS, suggests that "Unless we [gay couples] develop our own sense of community, we can burden our relationships with unrealistic expectations of what they are likely to provide for us."[89]

## What are our expectations?

_____

_____

_____

_____

_____

_____

_____

## Avoid relationship isolation.

Driggs and Finn contend that relationship isolation is present in the absence of same-sex friends. Many couples feel that these kinds of friendships are threatening to their relationship. Additionally, they hypothesize that this kind of isolation creates pseudo-intimacy between partners. When couples spend all of their time together, it can "discourage individual risk taking and block personal growth." Psychotherapeutic identification of pseudo-intimacy includes "dependency," "co-dependency," "enmeshment," or "relationship addiction."[90]

89. Isensee, p. 125.
90. Driggs, pp. 15, 135,-136.

The existence of pseudo-intimacy in a relationship initially depends on the sexual boundaries (or lack of) gay couples set for themselves prior to entering a commitment. Since gay men usually do not enter engagements, marital contracts or have to contend with the possibility of getting pregnant, nothing exists to distinguish these typical "bonds between heterosexual couples." The absence of these distinguishable features "can be a source of ambiguity" in their relationships. Isensee suggests that "If you have sex before you [gay men] become emotionally involved, it can be confusing trying to figure out what else you want from each other. You may end up sleeping together once or twice, and then feel awkward trying to redefine the relationship.[91]

Isensee believes it is helpful to establish some independence as a means of avoiding relationship isolation. "Maintaining a sense of yourself as an individual while still affirming the importance of your relationship is a significant task for any member of a couple. Men are socialized to function independently, so a male couple may have a difficult time finding the balance of "Who I am, who are you, and who are we together?" A sense of self allows a genuine exchange between you and your partner.[92] Tessina notes that lesbian couples should work to create space between themselves, clearly outline financial jobs, work toward a positive view of self, assign parenting guidelines, and seek ways to spark romance and sexual activity.[93]

91. Ibid., p.
92. Isensee, p. 8.
93. Tessina, p. 23.

# How do we isolate ourselves?

_____

_____

_____

_____

_____

_____

_____

_____

## Understand competition in your relationship.

Feelings of competition can occur in any couple. Two partners may compare sexual attractiveness, salaries, education, number of friends, physical strength, or numerous other attributes as a way of balancing power and status between them. Although such rivalries can occur in any relationship, they are more common in gay male couples. [94]

94. Driggs, p. 144.

# What do we compete for?

_____

_____

_____

_____

_____

_____

_____

_____

_____

## Define yourselves.

Finally, the labels used to identify a gay or lesbian's partner often reveal the hidden conflicts present. Berzon says that these labels fall into two categories, "...those meant to conceal the true nature of the relationship and those meant to reveal its true nature." She believes, "The problem is that concealment too often is not confined to those situations in which it is felt to be absolutely necessary. It becomes a way of life. We don't mean to, of course, but we do perpetuate a trivialized view of ourselves by reducing the single most important relationship in our life to the status of 'friend' or 'roommate.'"[95]

95. Berzon, p. 19.

## How will we refer to each other?

Work _____

_____

Home_____

_____

Public_____

_____

Other _____

_____

_____

_____

## Is it necessary to have an extended family?

A study accomplished by the California School of Professional
Psychology at Almeda found that the evidence of social support
for gay and lesbian couples was predictive of relationship quality.
The support came from friends more so than family and the
more the support was perceived from these sources, the higher
the relationship quality.[96] Tessina suggests that couples must
seek approval of their relationships so that their commitments in
turn will be healthier and happier.[97] "Togetherness is the primary
goal of a committed, long term relationship, but it is possible
for the two members of such a couple to be too involved with

---

96. George M. Cuesta-Aragon, "The Effect of Knowledge of Human Immunodeficiency Virus
   Infection on the Quality of Gay Male Relationships," (www.gay.net, 30 Mar. 1997)
97. Tessina, p. 26.

each other. If one partner actually lives vicariously through the other, the relationship is placed in great danger," according to psychotherapist and couples counselor Andrea P. Fulton, MFCC.[98] Driggs and Finn also point to the existence of a bi-cultural identity in homosexual relationships. "When one partner is more integrated in gay culture and the other is more integrated in the heterosexual culture, you have a cross-cultural relationship. Miscommunication and hurt feelings are likely, and are similar to those that might occur if the two of you were from different countries, each with its own customs and language. Bell and Weinberg affirm Harry's notion that the "vast differences in age, social class, ethnicity, etc. can create irresolvable tensions."[99]

## Who is in our support system?

Name                          Contact Information

_____          _____

_____          _____

_____          _____

_____          _____

_____          _____

_____          _____

_____          _____

98. U. White.
99. Driggs, p. 138.

## How do I develop family support?

Some significant research has been accomplished on the subject of gay and lesbian relationships. Kurdek has effectively collected and presented data on the historical development of these relationships in his article "Lesbian and Gay Couples." He reports that D.P McWhirter and A. M. Mattison first classified the maturation of gay relationships in six stages, which include; the blending, nesting, maintaining, building, releasing and renewing stages. Kurdek also mentions D. M. Clunis and G. D. Green's similar stages beginning with a pre-relationship phase and followed by romance, conflict, acceptance, commitment and collaboration stages.[100]

The best method for developing family support systems that represent the uniqueness of gay relationships is through other gay couples and their affirming biological families. These "families of choice" can be found among your circle of friends, open and affirming church congregations and support groups like PFLAG. Making the connections is the first step to developing an effective family support system.

## What are the organizations in our area that can help support our relationship?

100. Kurdek, p. 247.

May the sun
bring you new energy by day,

May the moon
softly restore you by night,

may the rain
wash away your worries

may the breeze
blow new strength into your being

may you walk
gently through the world and know
its beauty all the days of your life.

— apache blessing

# Conclusion

A note to the couple counselees:

I want you to read these words of affirmation to each other.

"You are loved by God, created in God's image, and blessed to live an authentic and abundant life. As a couple we are great together! No matter what our differences, prejudices, homophobic tendencies, identity issues, sex role socialization or family hang-ups, we can make it…together."

Today you begin, or perhaps rekindle, a new kind of life together; a life framed by a commitment to joy and happiness…a life grounded in God's love. This grounded love can grow and mature and endure, but only if you both determine to make it so. A lasting and growing love is never automatic, nor guaranteed by any ceremony. Let the foundation of your union be the pure love you have for each other, not just at this moment, but for all the days ahead. Honor faithfully the statements and commitments that you have brought to these counseling sessions. Faults will appear where now you find contentment, and wonder can be crushed by the routine of daily living. But today you resolve that your love will never be blotted out by the commonplace, obscured by the ordinary, or compromised by life's difficulties. Stand fast in that hope and confidence, and believe in your shared future just as strongly as you believe in yourselves and in each other today. Only in this spirit can you create a partnership that will sustain all the days of your lives. Celebrate this journey together.

And so it is!

# References and Resources

D'Augelli, Anthony R., and Charlotte Patterson, eds. *Lesbian, Gay, and Bisexual Identities Over the Lifespan: Psychological Perspectives* (Oxford: Oxford UP, 1995).

Bell, Alan P., Martin S. Weinberg, and Sue Kiefer Hammersmith. *Sexual Preference: Its Development in Men and Women* (Bloomington: Indiana UP, 1988).

Bell, Alan P., and Martin S. Weinberg. *Homosexualities: A Study of Diversity Among Men and Women* (NY: Simon & Schuster, 1979).

Berzon, Betty. *Permanent Partners: Building Gay & Lesbian Relationships That Last* (NY: Dutton, 2004).

Cuesta-Aragon, George M. "The Effect of Knowledge of Human Immunodeficiency Virus Infection on the Quality of Gay Male Relationships," (www.gay.net).

Davies, Dominic, and Charles Neal, Editors. *Pink Therapy: A Guide for counselors and Therapists Working with Lesbian, Gay, and Bisexual Clients* (Philadelphia: Open University Press, 1996).

*Dictionary of Pastoral Care and Counseling*, Rodney J. Hunter, General Editor (Nashville: Abingdon Press, 2005).

Driggs, John H., and Steven E. Finn. *Intimacy Between Men* (NY: Dutton-Penguin, 1991).

Fox, Sue. "The Ex-Files: When the Lovin' Ends, the Drama Begins," *Washington Blade*, 9 Aug. 1996.

Graham, Larry Kent. *Care of Persons, Care of Worlds* (Nashville: Abingdon Press, 1992).

Hancock, Kirstin A. "Psychotherapy with Lesbians and Gay Men," *Lesbian, Gay, and Bisexual Identities Over the Lifespan: Psychological Perspectives*, Anthony R. D'Augelli and Charlotte Patterson, eds. (Oxford: Oxford UP, 1995).

Hoffman, Wayne. "The Truest of Christian Struggles: Publications for Gay Christians' fight for Justice and Compassion," *Washington Blade*, 5 Jan. 1996.

Isensee, Rik. *Love Between Men: Enhancing Intimacy and Keeping Your Relationship Alive* (NY: Prentice Hall, 1992).

Jucha, Peter. "Gay is More Than Just Okay: Gay and Lesbian Persons Must Find a New Positive Theological Foundation for Their Lives," *Dallas Voice*, 7 Mar. 1997.

Kurdek, Lawrence. "Lesbian and Gay Couples," *Lesbian, Gay, and Bisexual Identities Over the Lifespan: Psychological Perspectives*, Anthony R. D'Augelli and Charlotte Patterson, eds. (Oxford: Oxford UP, 1995).

Marshall, Joretta L. *Counseling Lesbian Partners* (Louisville, KY: Westminster John Knox Press, 1997).

National Gay and Lesbian Task Force, "Get the NGLTF Action Kit on Same-Sex Marriages," (www.gay.net).

*PFLAG: Parents and Friends of Lesbians and Gays.* www.pflag.org

Peterson, Andrea L. T. "Dr. Richard Discusses the Value and Difficulties of Gay Relationships," *Dallas Voice*, 14 Jun. 1996.

*Reconciling Ministries Network.* www.rmnetwork.org

Scanzoni, Letha Dawson, and Virginia Ramey Mollenkott. *Is the Homosexual My Neighbor? : A Positive Christian Response* (NY: Harpercollins, 1994).

Spong, John Shelby. *Living in Sin?: A Bishop Rethinks Human Sexuality* (San Francisco: Harper, 1990).

Switzer, David K. *Pastoral Care of Gays, Lesbians, and Their Families* (Minneapolis: Fortress Press, 1999).

Tessina, Tina. *Gay Relationships* (NY: Putnam, 1990).

Vaillancourt, Daniel. "Berzon Counsels Couples for the Long Haul with The Intimacy Dance," *Dallas Voice*, 23 Aug. 1996.

Wallace, Elizabeth. "Berzon Hopes to Help Couples Commit For Life," *Washington Blade*, 22 Nov. 1996.

White, Edmund. *States of Desire: Travels in Gay America* (NY: Penguin, 1991), p. xiv.

White, Uneeda. "Therapists Discuss Finding a Balance in Lesbian and Gay Unions," *Dallas Voice*, 28 Feb. 1997.

# *Union Ceremony*
for

_____ & _____

_____,\_\_\_\_\_, 20\_\_\_\_ @ \_\_\_:\_\_\_\_ p.m.

Officiated by Reverend _____

Location _____

## *Prelude*
## *Processional*
## *Greeting*

**Pastor:** The grace of our Lord Jesus Christ and the love of God and the communion of the Holy Spirit be with you all.
**All:** And also with you.

## *Introduction*

We gather at the invitation of _____ and _____ to celebrate their love and commitment in a service to worship God, who blesses all that is good within us. Our most intimate relations are invitations into a spirituality of love, whether between a human being and God, a parent and a child, among believers or between lovers. God gives us this love. Through that love, partners come to know each other with mutual care and companionship. God gives joy. Through that joy, partners may share their new life with others. Therefore it is appropriate that we lift to God and to the families of our choosing, this couple in a public affirmation of their intimacy for each other. In a world where love may be offered without commitment and commitments may be made without love, we give thanks to God, whose own steadfast love inspires the union of these souls.

115

## Acknowledgement of Family and Friends

Today, in front of friends and family, they honor their commitment to not just gaze at one another, but to look outward together in the same direction. Today _____ and _____, proclaim their love to the world, and we rejoice with and for them. An important part of this affirmation of love is the recognition of family and friends who have come to embrace and sanction their union.

## The Rose Gift

This ceremony is also a celebration of family. It is the blending of two families, separate up to this moment, but united from this day forward -- blending their different traditions, strengthening the family tree. Parents plant so that their children may harvest. _____ and _____ wish to honor this blending of the families by presenting a rose to their parents -- to thank them for the many selfless sacrifices they have made and for their unconditional love so freely given to their children.

## Prayer

### In Unison

Gracious God, always faithful in your love for us, we rejoice in your presence. You create love. You unite us in one human family. You offer your word and lead us in light. You open your loving arms and embrace us with strength. May your presence fill our hearts with new joy and make new the lives of your children whose commitment we celebrate. Bless all creation through this sign of your love shown in the love of _____ and _____ for each other. May the power of your Spirit sustain them and all of us in love that knows no end. Amen.

# *Scripture Reading*

*(Choose one or more of these scripture passages, or suggest your favorites from other sacred texts. You also might suggest a family member or friend to read them.)*

| Old Testament Reading | Epistles | Gospel Reading |
|---|---|---|
| Genesis 1:26-28, 31 | Romans 8:31-39 | Matthew 5:1-12 |
| Genesis 2: 18-24 | Romans 8:1-2, 9-18 | Matthew 5:13-16 |
| Ruth 1:16-18 | | Matthew 7:21, 24-29 |
| Psalm 23, 33, 34, 37, 67, 100, 103, 112, 117, 121, 127, 128, 136, 145, 148, 150 | I Corinthians 6:15-20 | Matthew 19:3-6 |
| | I Corinthians 13:1-13 | Matthew 22:35-40 |
| Song of Solomon 2:8-13 | Ephesians 3:14-21 | Mark 10:6-9 |
| | Ephesians 5:2, 21-33 | Mark 10:13-16 |
| Isaiah 54:5-8 | | John 2:1-11 |
| Jeremiah 31:31-34 | Colossians 3:12-17 | John 15:9-17 |
| Hosea 2:16-23 | I Peter 3:1-9 | |
| | I John 3:18-24 | |
| | I John 4:7-16 | |
| | Revelation 19:1, 5-9 | |

# *Homily*

Reverend _____

If we had to describe God in one word, it would be this: God is Love. If we had only one sentence to express the essence of the Gospel, the Good News of Jesus, the Christ, it would be this: You are loved. If we had only one command that would enable the realization of this love in our lives, it would be this: Love each other.

Many throughout the ages have explored what it means to love and be loved. And many can offer to us the wisdom they have discovered from seasoned experience. The love of which they and I speak today is Holy Love. It is Holy Love that brings us to this hopeful place. It is Holy Love that we celebrate and bless this day.

Holy Love is an essential gift. It's not a commodity that can be bought or earned, or even fully deserved. In its essence, it is gift. It is grace. And our deepest response to such love is gratitude and thanks.

The Holy Love of which I speak is also insightful. The lover can see in the other the potential the other cannot see in herself/himself, and accepts the vocation to call out that beauty—to call out that potential from the other.

Holy Love is radically merciful and forgiving. It willingly offers release from the burdensome baggage of the past and it offers the possibility to begin again—and again—and again.

Holy Love is sacrificial, willing to place the welfare of the other even above our own.

Holy Love is self-giving—facing outward. It believes that together, two people can love the world in a way that cannot be done so separately.

This Holy Love is always justice-seeking. It is a tough love, willing to confront the inequities and injustices that inevitably exist in any relationship. It always seeks peace and perfect harmony.

During this controversial time of affirmation of same-sex relationships the Defense of Marriage Act has dominated the religious and political climate. As a minister I am motivated to continually seek justice for gay and lesbian relationships by the journey that Jesus took to Jerusalem during Holy Week, the period between Palm and Easter Sundays, to confront the Powers-That-Be.

Throughout his life, Jesus takes the time to heal the sick, minister to the outcast and the marginalized, and break bread with all kinds of folks whom others disdain and oppress. But he doesn't simply touch and heal and minister and break bread with those who are marginalized. He also calls into question the systems that allow some "in" and keep some "out." Time and time again, in each of the gospels, Jesus is portrayed challenging the Roman occupation and the religious authorities who oppress. It is to offer this challenge that he goes to Jerusalem, the seat of power—at the beginning of what we call, "Holy Week."

"Can we make this journey with Jesus?" "Can we move toward the Jerusalems in our lives and confront the Powers-That-Be?" "Do we have the courage and the strength, to risk oppression— and sometimes even crucifixion?" These questions are amazingly apt today—particularly for those who are lesbian, gay, bisexual and transgender and for those who are allies.

There are no easy answers. For like the journey that Jesus took toward his Jerusalem, our choices involve risking ourselves. For some it means coming out. For others it means sacrificing time and energy. For still others, it means speaking truth to those who might respond with condemnation. As we struggle with these realities, we remember the crucified one. But we also remember that crucifixion was not the end of the journey. Resurrection was! And that is the ground of all of our intimate journeys. Although we must engage the Powers-That-Be; although such confrontation is risky and, indeed, death- dealing at times; although we are scared and can lose hope—the final word is always God's desire for making love and life abundant.

_____ and _____, this Holy Love of which I speak is the mystery of God's love, embodied in the Christian tradition as Jesus the Christ. As you celebrate your love this day, I challenge and encourage you to love each other—and to love the world and all you meet therein—with Holy Love.

## Declaration of Commitment

_____ and _____, in presenting yourselves here today you perform a remarkable act of faith. This faith can grow and mature and endure, but only if you both determine to make it so. A lasting and growing love is never automatic, nor guaranteed by any ceremony. Let the foundation of your union be the pure love you have for each other, not just at this moment, but for all the days ahead, honor faithfully the statements and commitments that you bring here today. Faults will appear where now you find contentment, and wonder can be crushed by the routine of daily living. But today you resolve that your love will never be blotted out by the commonplace, obscured by the ordinary, or compromised by life's difficulties. Stand fast in that hope and confidence, and believe in your shared future just as strongly as you believe in yourselves and in each other today. Only in this spirit can you create a partnership that will sustain all the days of your lives.

_____ and _____, we are here to celebrate as you begin this journey together It is in this spirit that you have come here to today to exchange these vows.

# Pledge of Support

**Addressing the Families:** Will the families of
_____ and _____.
both biological families and families of choice, please stand and
answer in support of this couple. Do you offer your prayerful
blessing and loving support to this union?

Please answer, "We do."

**Addressing the Whole Gathering:** Do you, as children
of God, pledge your support and encouragement to the
covenant commitment that _____ and
_____are making together?

Please answer, "We do."

# Vows of the Union

_____ and _____.
by your covenant promises shared with us today, you unite
yourselves in a union of Holy Love and subject yourselves to
each other as partners for life.

_____, please read your vows:

(Sample vows, please write your own when possible!)
*From this day forward I promise you these things. I will laugh with you
in times of joy and comfort you in times of sorrow. I will share in your
dreams, and support you as you strive to achieve your goals. I will listen to
you with compassion and understanding, and speak lovingly to you with
encouragement. I will help you when you need it, and step aside when you
don't. I will remain faithful to you for better or worse, in times of sickness
and health.*

_____, please read your vows:

*You are my best friend. I promise to encourage and inspire you, to laugh with you, and to comfort you in times of sorrow and struggle. I promise to love you in good times and in bad, when life seems easy and when it seems hard, when our love is simple, and when it is an effort. These things I give to you today, and all the days of our life.*

## Exchange of Rings

_____ and _____.

please receive your rings. Rings are made precious by our wearing of them. Your rings say that even in your uniqueness you have chosen to be bound together. Let these rings also be a sign that love has substance as well as soul, a present as well as a past, and that, despite its occasional sorrows, love is a circle of happiness, wonder, and delight.

_____, take this ring and place it on
_____'s finger and repeat after me:

*With this ring I take you to be my best friend, lover, and partner for life.*

_____, take this ring and put it on
_____'s finger, and repeat after me:

*With this ring I take you to be my best friend, lover, and partner for life.*

## Sand Ceremony

The sand ceremony represents leaving your two separate lives and joining to make one life together. Your separate lives are symbolized by two vases of sand, in different colors. To grow a relationship requires more than just two people. It requires the love, support and encouragement of family members, extended family and friends. I now ask your parents to pour their individual vases of sand into _____ and
_____'s

central vase as the foundation for this commitment.

_____ and _____
will now pour their individual vases into the central vase.

The third component of your relationship is the presence of
the Holy Spirit. Symbolized by the red sand poured into the top
of the vase, we ask the Holy Spirit to pour into each of you;
that your relationship becomes the living vessel of God's grace
and love. We ask You, Holy Spirit to guide them, protect them,
comfort them, and nurture them in their new life together.

_____ and _____.
you have just performed your first spiritual ritual as a deeply
committed couple. Your newly formed union and the union
of your two families, is represented by this intertwined pattern
of sand you have created. Just as you could no longer separate
the newly formed pattern into individual grains, so are you now
joined together. This symbol is a keepsake of your commitment
ceremony and reminds you that from this moment on, you are
one family, anchored in love.

## *Pronouncement of Union*

_____ and _____.
you have shown today by these words which were spoken, that
your hearts and souls were destined to be joined. So, by joining
hands now and looking into each other's eyes, let it be known that
you are joined, body and soul in this lifetime. And now that you
have exchanged these vows, it gives me gives me great pleasure to
pronounce that you are and will continue to be partners for life.
You may seal your Union with a kiss.

# Benediction

May the wings of angels uphold you through all the life of your love, may you live forever in happiness with one another. May your hearts be full; may you lips stay sweet. May your love grow strong; may you love long and happily in one another's arms.

**All:** Amen!

Now family and friends, it is with great honor I present to you a very loving and committed couple, and one that is beloved by God. Let us celebrate

_____ and _____.


# Recessional